M000287886

Winter Whimsy

Creative Clip Art for Classroom & Home
Created & Designed by Dianne J. Hook

ISBN 1-59441-178-6

Contents

Credits

Illustrator: Dianne J. Hook
Content Design and Project Director: Sherrill B. Flora
Editor: Karen Seberg
Production: Mark Conrad
Cover Production: Annette Hollister-Papp

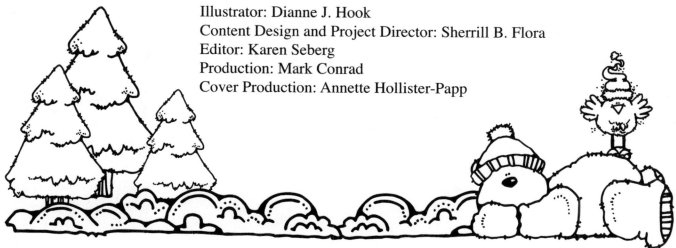

Clip Art Assembly Basics

Here are some suggestions as you make your flyers, announcements, or any project using clip art from this book.

Tools

Putting together the right tools will make your project go more smoothly and look better in the end. A good copy machine is a must. It's worth the extra effort to make sure your school or copy shop has machines that make clean copies. You will also need a bottle of white paper correction fluid, a fine-tip black marker to combine designs and add your own art to the project, rubber cement to mount the design on paper during the layout stage of your project, and scissors for cutting apart the designs you choose. Optional tools to help create a professional-looking project are a nonreproducible blue pencil to make marks that will not show up on copies, a proportion scale to help you determine the size of the reduction or enlargement necessary to fit your paper, and blue grid paper for laying out the project with straight lines.

Assembly Steps

1. Choose the design or designs you will be putting together for the project that you will be making.

2. Copy the design once from the book so that you have a copy from which to work without having to cut apart your book.

3. Cut out the designs from your copy and lay them out on your paper. (Blue grid paper comes in handy.) A light table can also help with the layout of your page.

4. Next, make a copy of the designs and any text on the paper before adding any other hand-drawn illustrations. Drawing over the grid paper lines is difficult and generally doesn't turn out well.

5. Now you have a good idea of what your project is going to look like. Go ahead and add all the extra finishing touches. Small doodles or even simple dots or squares can really "warm up" the page and keep it from looking choppy.

6. Make your final copies of the page. Easy!

Hints

* Keep a 1-inch (0.6 cm) margin on all edges of your paper.
* If the edges of the cutout pieces are visible on your copies, lighten the copy machine one notch or use correction fluid on one copy and then use it to make the final copies.
* Removable tape is great for creating layouts if you will be using the design more than once.

Have fun! You can become an artist and create wonderful projects for your class with the help of this book!

December

4

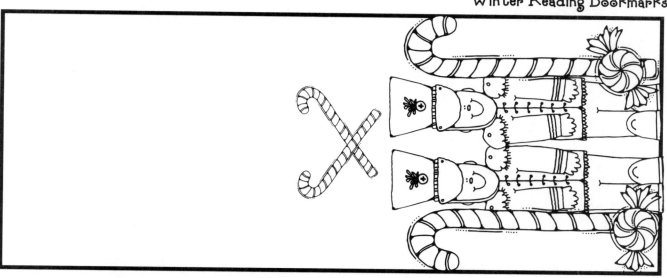

Winter Reading

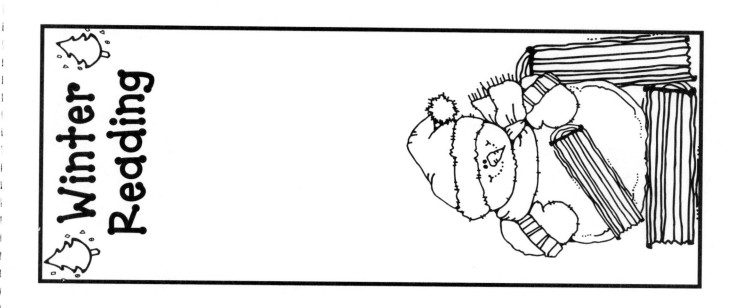

December
Classroom
Helpers

just for you!

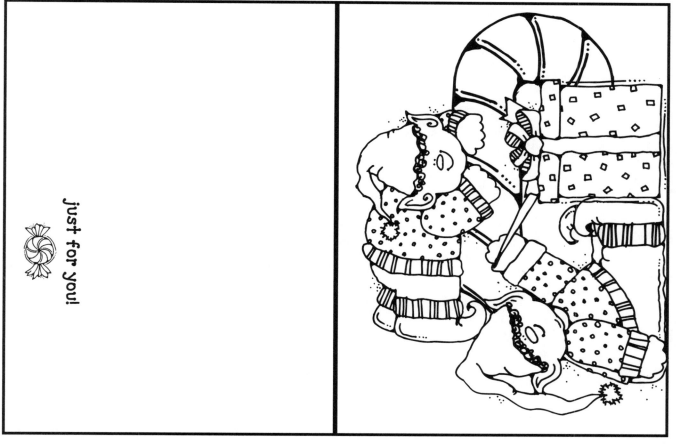

just for you!

 Happy Holidays

Joy

"Bah, humbug!"

Peace

Happy Holly Days

Season's Greetings

Greetings from your teacher

Holiday Happiness

Christmas Cheer

A Season for Giving

HO HO HO

"Making a list... checking it twice!"

No
peekin'!

Just
for
YOU!

'Tis
the
Season

14

A note to parents...

15

Happy Hanukkah

Happy Hanukkah

Festival of Lights

19

20

Dear Santa,

December News

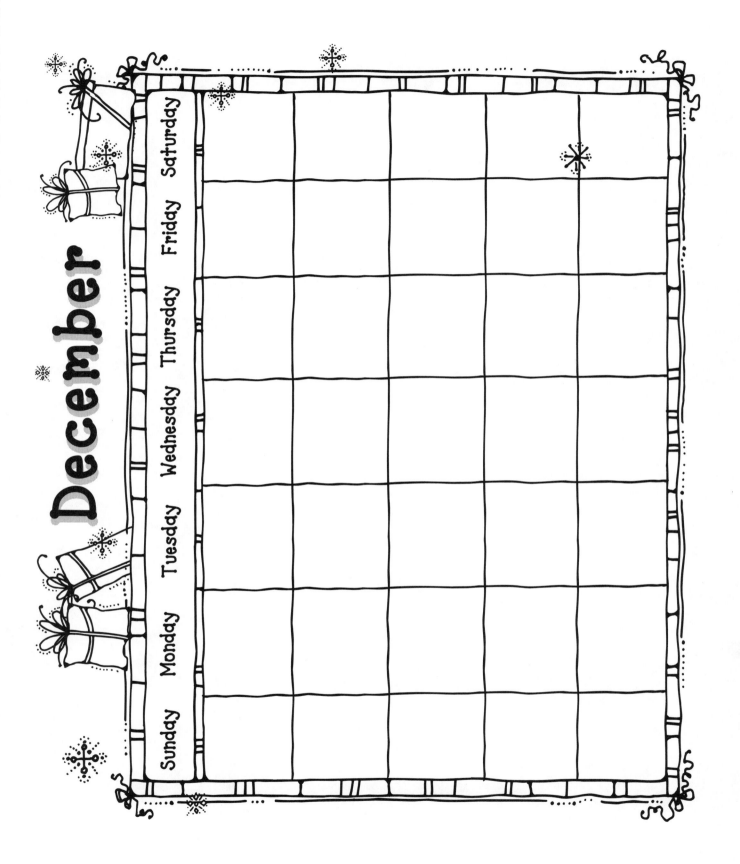

December

Sunday	Monday	Tuesday	Wednesday	Thursday	Friday	Saturday

January

Hooray for YOU!

Winter Fun

28

January Birthday List

Brrr! It's COLD!

Snowflakes and Smiles

Happy New Year!

YOU did it!

Great big THANKS!

WINTER NEWS

Spelling List

Homework

Hall Pass

Library Pass

Student of the Month

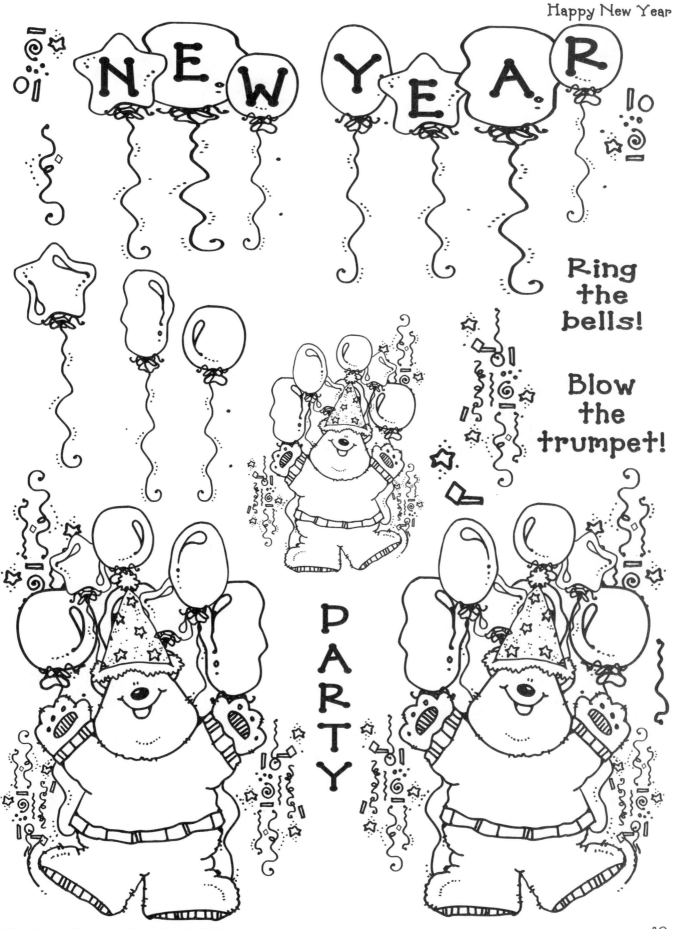

NEW YEAR

Ring
the
bells!

Blow
the
trumpet!

PARTY

Happy New Year!

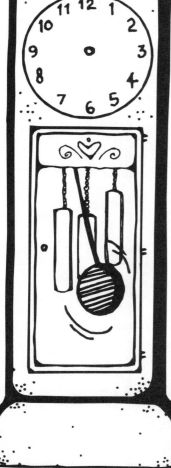

Out with the old... in with the new!

My resolutions...

Our class is COOL!

Warm toes and tummies

33

Winter

Happy New Year!

NEWS!

36

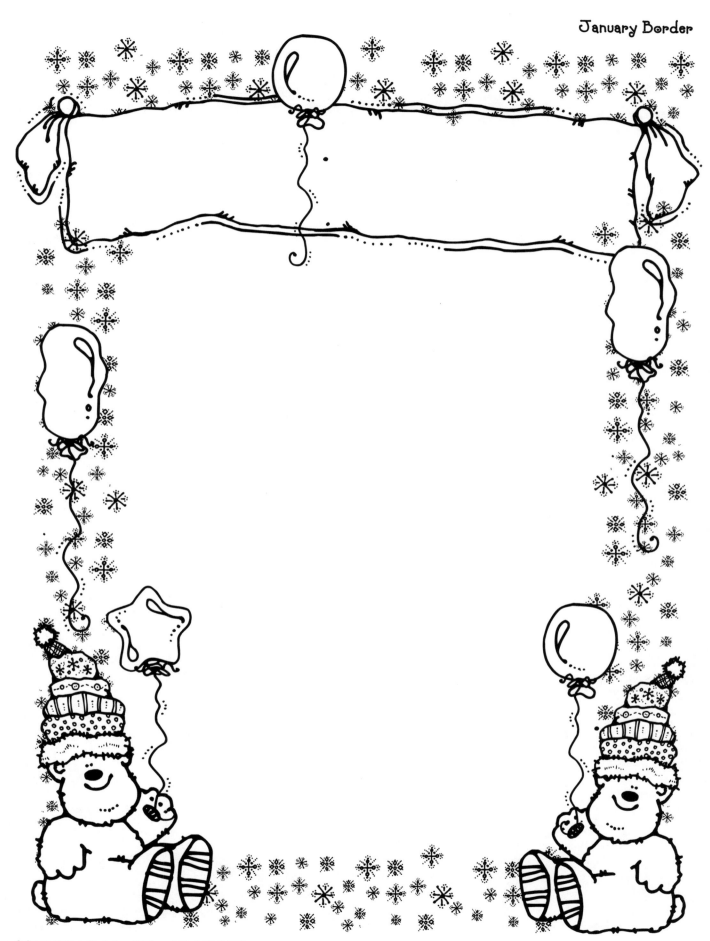

37

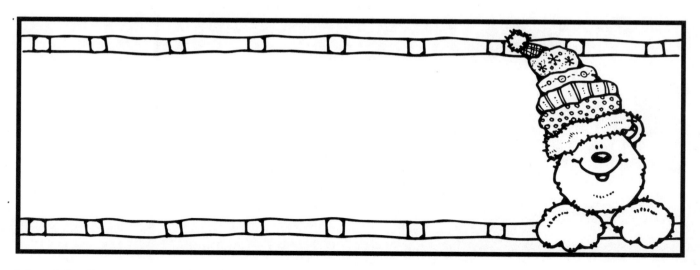

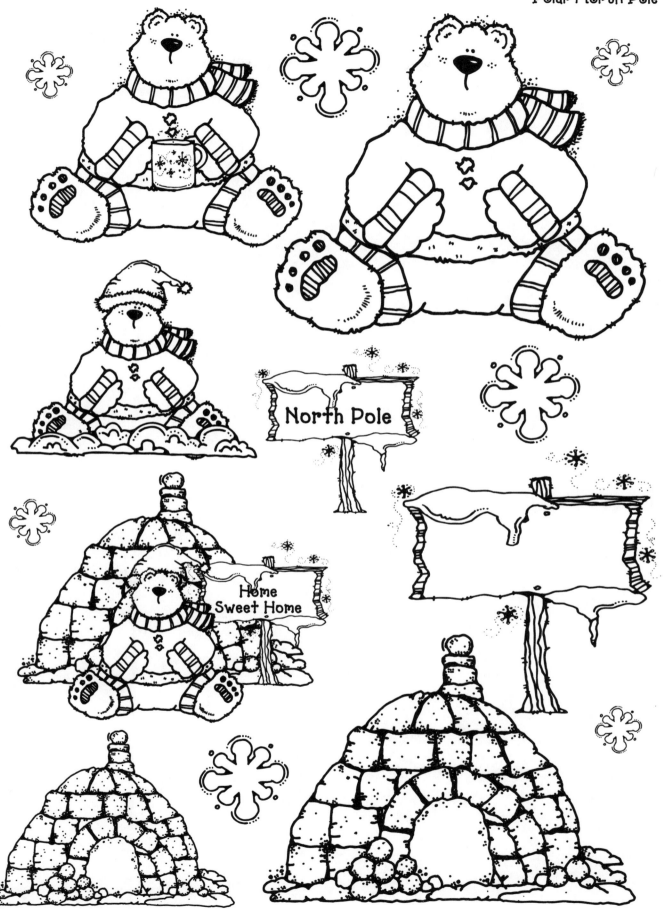

North Pole

Home
Sweet Home

40

It's snow time!

LET IT SNOW

41

January News

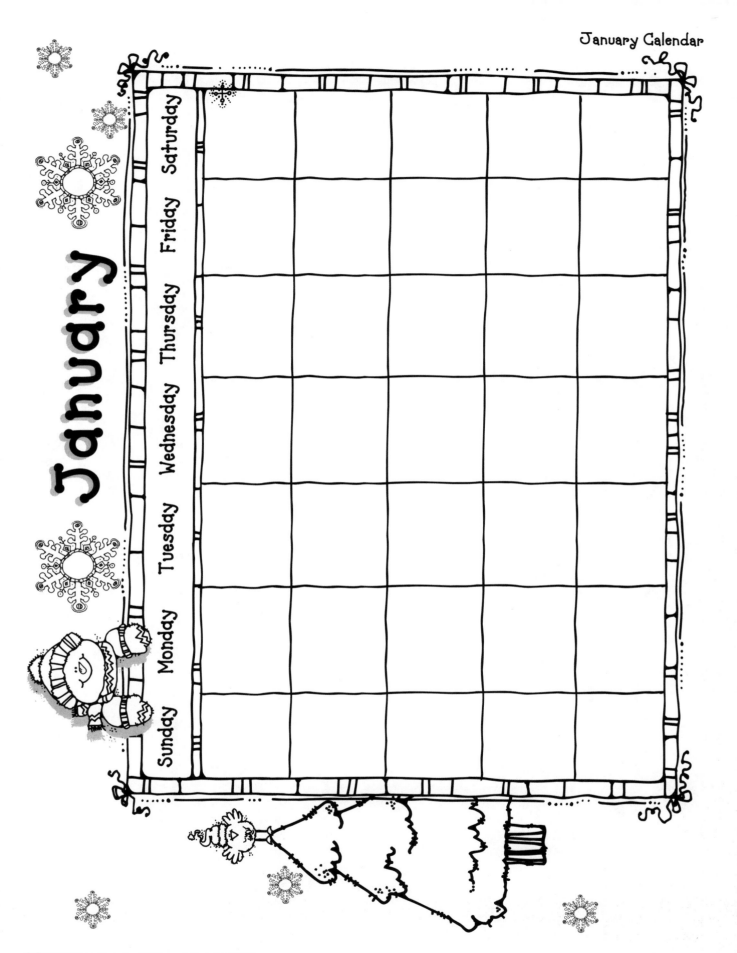

February

Bake Sale!

Just for you!

Be my valentine.

Thinking of YOU!

Valentine's Day Party!

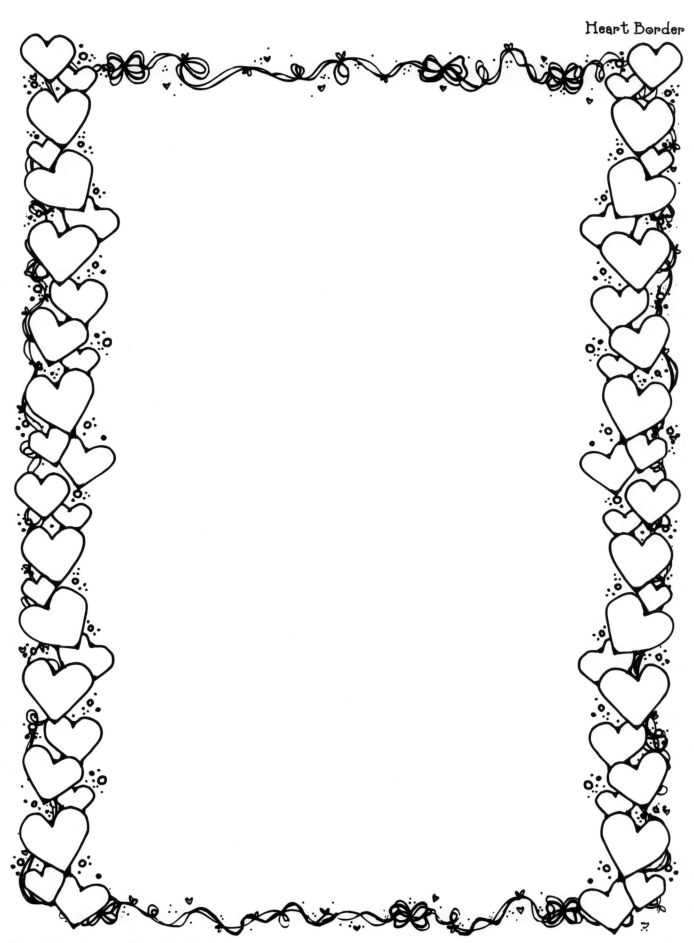

From the Heart

Just a Note

Thank You

Presidents' Day!

Founding Father

December

January

February

Love Note...

Happy Heart Day!

No "LION,"
You're the best,
Valentine!

Be Mine...

Valentine's Hugs!

You're Special!

FOR YOU

February News

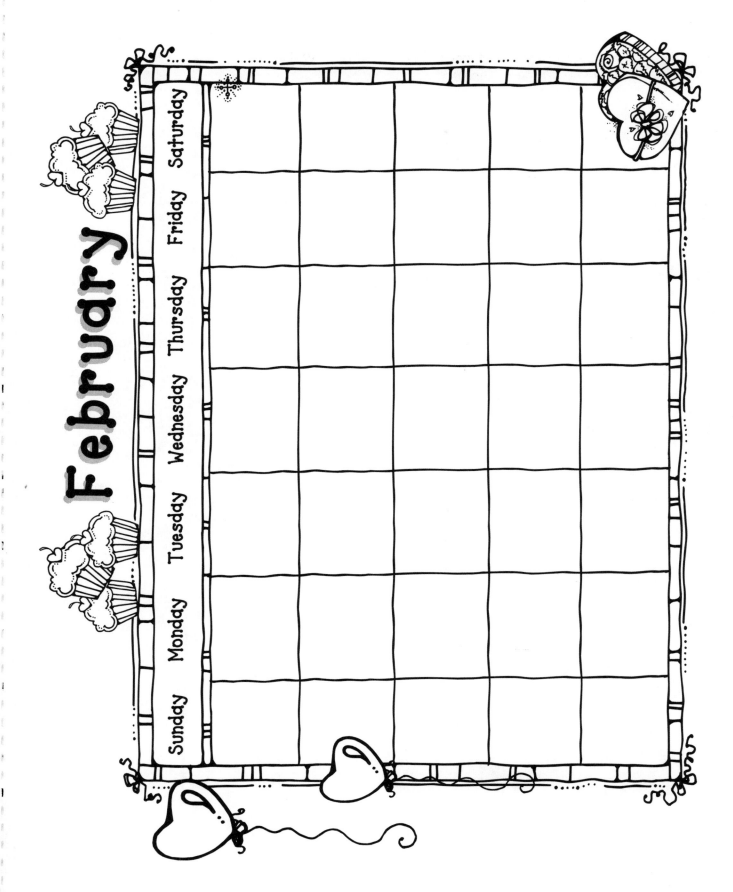

February

Sunday	Monday	Tuesday	Wednesday	Thursday	Friday	Saturday